★ *GREAT SPORTS TEAMS* ★

THE MIAMI

DOLPHINS

FOOTBALL TEAM

J.J. DiLorenzo

Enslow Publishers, Inc.

44 Fadem Road	PO Box 38
Box 699	Aldershot
Springfield, NJ 07081	Hants GU12 6BP
USA	UK

Library of Congress Cataloging-in-Publication Data

DiLorenzo, J.J.
    The Miami Dolphins football team / J.J. DiLorenzo.
        p. cm. — (Great sports teams)
    Includes bibliographical references (p.) and index.
    Summary: Covers the history of the record-setting Miami Dolphins,
discussing some key players, coaches, and important games.
    ISBN 0-89490-796-4
    1. Miami Dolphins (Football team)—History—Juvenile literature. [1. Miami
Dolphins (Football team) 2. Football—History.] I. Title. II. Series.
GV956.M47D55 1997
796.332'64'09759381—dc20   96-26414
                                                                      CIP
                                                                       AC

Printed in the United States of America

10 9 8 7 6 5 4 3 2 1

Illustration Credits: AP/Wide World Photos, pp. 4, 7, 8, 10, 13, 14, 16, 19, 20, 22, 25, 26, 28, 31, 32, 34, 37, 39.

Cover Illustration: AP/Wide World Photos.

CONTENTS

*A*lways determined, Larry Csonka bulls through the Pittsburgh defense to gain some yardage. The Dolphins beat the Steelers 21–17 in the 1972 AFC Championship Game.

PERFECT SEASON

A record crowd at the Los Angeles Memorial Coliseum was electrified.[1] By the time the football game started, the tension and excitement had risen to a peak.

The Miami Dolphins and the Washington Redskins were about to face off in Super Bowl VII, on January 14, 1973. This would be the most significant Super Bowl game in history—if the Dolphins won—because it would practically guarantee a never-to-be broken record.

Setting a Record

No National Football League (NFL) team had ever had an undefeated, untied regular season topped off with undefeated playoff games—no team, that is, until the Miami Dolphins did it in 1972. Having won all fourteen regular season games, they continued their winning ways into postseason play. They beat the Cleveland

Browns, 20–14, in the American Football Conference (AFC) playoff game, then took care of the Pittsburgh Steelers, 21–17, for the AFC championship.

The big question now was: Could the Dolphins stretch their undefeated season to seventeen straight victories? Football fans everywhere could only marvel at the possibility of such an outcome.

If the Dolphins won The Big One, they would become the only NFL team with an undefeated, untied season and postseason, as well as a Super Bowl win. Their victory would be the most precedent-shattering and record-setting game in the history of the NFL! Could they do it?

Super Bowl VII

The Washington Redskins, with their season record of 11-3, and their title game win of 26–3 against the tough Dallas Cowboys, would not be an easy mark.[2] Don Shula's well-oiled Miami machine was ready for the confrontation.

The Dolphins had a talent-laden offense that included subsequent Hall of Famers: quarterback Bob Griese, fullback Larry Csonka, center Jim Langer, guard Larry Little, and wide receiver Paul Warfield.

The Dolphins' underrated No-Name Defense, without a Hall of Fame player among them, was an outstanding unit that superbly complemented the offense. Middle linebacker Nick Buoniconti, defensive linemen Manny Fernandez and Bill Stanfill, and safeties Jake Scott and Dick Anderson would prove that they were up to the challenge.

The Dolphins' Jim Kiick (21) puts his head down and runs for the goal. Kiick scored the touchdown that gave the Dolphins the early lead in Super Bowl VII.

First Half

From the time the game began it was a defensive stalemate until late in the first period, when Bob Griese, at the 28-yard line, gunned a pass to wide receiver Howard Twilly at the 5. Twilly quickly scored, and kicker Garo Yepremian kicked the ball through the goal posts to give the Dolphins the lead, 7–0.

Miami scored again in the second period. This time the play was set up by linebacker Nick Buoniconti's 32-yard interception return. Griese's 19-yard pass to tight end Jim Mandich brought the ball to the 2. After the touchdown was made by running back Jim Kiick, Yepremian's successful kick made the score 14–0.

*T*he Dolphins' Manny Fernandez (75) stops the Redskins' Larry Brown dead in his tracks. The Dolphins held on to win Super Bowl VII 14–7, finishing their season undefeated.

Second Half

In the second half, both defensive teams played extremely well. Neither side scored in the third period, and the score remained 14–0. It wasn't until the end of the fourth quarter that the Redskins finally scored a touchdown in what the Dolphins themselves called a bizarre play.

It wasn't so bad that Yepremian's attempted long field goal was blocked, but when he recovered the ball, he foolishly attempted a pass. The ball rolled off his fingers into the hands of Washington's defensive back Mike Bass, who ran 49 yards for a Redskins touchdown. With a successful kick, the score became 14–7.

Fortunately, when Miami got the kickoff with only about two minutes left to play, they were able to run out the clock. Ironically, the freak play kept the Miami defense from enjoying a shutout.[3] Nevertheless, the bottom line was that Miami won the Super Bowl, for its seventeenth straight win!

Happy Ending

With the victory, Don Shula became the only coach in the NFL to have a 17-0 season. He said it all when he said, "This is the ultimate."[4]

The year 1972 was a significant season not only for the Miami Dolphins and Coach Don Shula, but also for the NFL; the 17-0 season record is still unbroken.

*T*his 1965 news conference announced that Miami would have a professional football team. Seated left to right are Miami Mayor Robert King, AFL Commissioner Joe Foss, and Joe Robbie.

A TEAM FOR MIAMI

In 1965, lawyer Joe Robbie applied for a football franchise for Miami. Obtaining financial backing and assurance that the team could play in the Orange Bowl, he got the Miami mayor to invite the American Football League (AFL) to the city. In June of the following year, the AFL awarded its first expansion franchise to Miami, and the Dolphins were born.[1]

Rough Start

Everyone expects a new expansion team to lose during its first few seasons, which is exactly what the Miami Dolphins did. Their record in their first four years was a dismal 3-11, 4-10, 5-8-1 (tie), and 3-10-1.[2]

It was easy to forget that the team's first coach George Wilson didn't have too much to work with. Coming from eight creditable years with the Detroit

Lions, he now had to work with a bunch of rookies and several NFL players past their prime.

For four years he drafted and traded, but somehow the team never gelled. Understandably, the fans were getting impatient. For too long, the only cheering action on the field came from Flipper, the live dolphin mascot, who was kept in a pool at one end of the stadium. Meanwhile, the team kept losing, the fans stayed away, and even Flipper lost his job because he was too expensive.

Shula's Early Years

In 1970, the first year of the completed merger of the AFL and NFL, the Dolphins were entering their new league from a consistently losing position. Something had to be done to get the team on track. That something was a new coach, Don Shula.

Coming from a successful stint as coach of the Baltimore Colts, Shula claimed, "I don't have a magic formula,"[3] but no one would believe it based on the results. "I'm about as subtle as a punch in the mouth,"[4] he said, and he proved it, not by waving a magic wand, but by working the tails off the players.

Getting on Track

Under Shula's leadership, the team won four games in a row in preseason play. By sticking to a vigorous training schedule, the Dolphins began to get their act together. With the first eight games of the regular

Quarterback George Wilson, Jr., talks things over with his father, head coach George Wilson, Sr., during the 1966 season. The team started poorly, finishing 3–11 in their first season.

season split, Miami went on to win each of the final six games.[5] Not bad for a team that had finished the previous year in the cellar of the Eastern Division.

Thanks to Coach Shula, the perennial losing streak of the Miami Dolphins came to an end. He finished his first year with a 10-4 record, second only to the Baltimore Colts' 11-2-1. More significantly, the team won a wildcard slot against the Oakland Raiders. Though Oakland won that game 21–14, the Dolphins had proved they were on the way up—and up they went.

A Team for Miami

*A*fter the 1969 season George Wilson was replaced by former Baltimore Colts coach Don Shula. Shula had led the Baltimore Colts into Super Bowl III where they fell to the New York Jets.

Making History

The Dolphins continued their winning ways through 1971, when they had a 10-3-1 season, earning the Eastern Division title. They played Kansas City in the conference playoff in the longest game in NFL history: eighty-two minutes and forty seconds.

With the score tied 24–24 at the end of regulation time, the game went into overtime. At 7:40 into the second overtime, Garo Yepremian booted a 37-yard field goal, winning the game 27–24.[6] The Dolphins then went on to win the championship against Baltimore.

In just six short years, and only two under Shula, the Dolphins were on their way to Super Bowl VI. Unfortunately, they lost to the Dallas Cowboys, 24–3. Still, this was only the second time in the Dolphins' short history that they had a winning season and their first time ever in the Super Bowl.

Back in the locker room, undaunted by the loss, Coach Shula told his players, "We have to dedicate ourselves to getting back to the Super Bowl next season and winning it."[7] With those marching orders, the coach's single-mindedness, and the team's hard work, it all came together in 1972: an unprecedented undefeated season.

At last Miami fans had something to cheer about.

*I*n 1967, Bob Griese joined the Miami Dolphins as a rookie. He would go on to win almost seventy percent of the games he participated in, and was inducted into the Pro Football Hall of Fame in 1990.

STAR PLAYERS

A mong the most talented acquisitions in the Dolphins' early years were Bob Griese, Larry Csonka, Larry Little, Paul Warfield, and Jim Langer. These players, all subsequent Hall of Famers, were instrumental in achieving Miami's phenomenal success in the early 1970s.

Bob Griese

The Dolphins' precision offense revolved around quarterback Bob Griese, who was a natural leader.[1] His remarkable intelligence and acute instincts earned him the reputation as the "thinking man's quarterback."[2] Although he was not one of the biggest quarterbacks, what Griese lacked in size he more than made up for in brains.[3]

Called upon as a rookie to complete the opening game of 1967 when John Stofa broke his ankle, Griese calmly and coolly stepped in and directed the team to a

35–21 win over the Denver Broncos. Griese continued to excel, becoming the fourteenth passer in the NFL's highly selective five-thousand yard club. Owner Joe Robbie, noting Griese's .698 winning percentage (91-39-1), called him "the cornerstone of the franchise."[4]

Larry Csonka

The workhorse of the Dolphins' offense was running back Larry Csonka. Csonka resented being called a bulldozer because he knew that running backs had to be intelligent. They had to recognize and quickly react to the different situations that occurred with every play.[5] As proof that he was more than a mindless hulk, Csonka could point to his ranking as the Dolphins' all-time leading rusher with 1,506 carries for 6,737 yards and 53 touchdowns (TDs).

Larry Little

Guard Larry Little was another key ingredient of the Dolphins' back-to-back Super Bowl Championship teams of 1972 and 1973. During the 1970s, he was an intimidating force in a Miami running attack that led the NFL at 2,372 yards per season. He was the first player in league history to be named AFC Offensive Lineman of the Year for three straight seasons.

Paul Warfield

Wide receiver Paul Warfield had 156 receptions for 3,355 yards and 33 TDs in his five seasons with the Dolphins. At that time, Warfield was the only Dolphin in the team's history to score 4 touchdowns in one game.

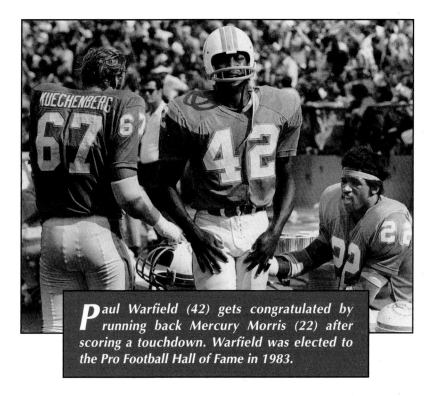

***P**aul Warfield (42) gets congratulated by running back Mercury Morris (22) after scoring a touchdown. Warfield was elected to the Pro Football Hall of Fame in 1983.*

Jim Langer

During the team's championship years of the early 1970s, Jim Langer was the anchor of the Miami offensive line. He holds the distinction of having played every offensive down in the Dolphins' perfect 1972 season. During his career, he also set team records for playing in 128 straight games and for having 109 consecutive starts.

Earl Morrall

Although he is not a Hall of Famer, mention must be made of the unsung hero of the winning 1972 season, quarterback Earl Morrall. He took over for the injured

*D*ropping back to pass, Dan Marino tries to spot an open receiver. Marino holds many records including most completions, most yards passing, and most touchdown passes.

Bob Griese in the scoreless fifth game of the season, and led the team to a 24–10 win. He also spearheaded the wins in every remaining game of the regular season.

Dan Marino

No listing of great Dolphins would be complete without the sensational quarterback Dan Marino. Although Miami had a top-notch team in 1982, it did not have a first-rate quarterback—until Marino was drafted in 1983. After superbly playing relief in the third and fifth games of his first NFL season, Marino started—and completed—the sixth game and every game thereafter.

From his first appearance in 1983, when he completed 11 of 17 passes for 90 yards and 2 scores, to the last game of the 1995 regular season, Marino has excelled in every category. Through the 1995 season, Marino completed 3,931 of 6,531 passes for 48,841 yards and 352 TD passes, surpassing the NFL records set by Fran Tarkenton in each of those categories.

Marino, named 1983 NFL Rookie of the Year, was the first rookie quarterback starter in a Pro Bowl, and has been selected to play in nine Pro Bowls. Marino has won the AFC Offensive Player of the Week honor fifteen times in regular seasons and twice in postseason games.

"There is no doubt that Marino is the greatest pure passer ever to play the game," pronounced Edwin Pope, a veteran Miami sportswriter.

Unquestionably a future Hall of Famer, Marino has time to break even more records.

*J*oe Robbie founded the Miami Dolphins franchise. In 1987, Robbie announced the opening of Joe Robbie Stadium, where the Dolphins would now play their home games.

BUILDING THE TEAM

Many teams can review their history and identify the several owners and two or three coaches who really made a difference. The Dolphins have only to look back to their first owner and their coach of twenty-six years to identify the men who put them in the record books.

Joe Robbie

Joe Robbie was the driving force behind getting a football franchise for Miami.[1] He was also responsible for building the Dolphins a new stadium, without which the team might have moved to another city. Most appropriately, it is named Joe Robbie Stadium.[2]

Although owners clearly influence the course of their teams, ultimately the coaches are the individuals who bear the responsibility for the teams' victories and defeats.

Don Shula

When he went to Miami in 1970, Shula's job was to turn Miami's individual players into a disciplined, cohesive, and winning team. In his first year, beyond the most optimistic expectations, he did just that: the team had its very first winning season. He didn't just win his first season, he was a consistent winner.

The Working Duo

Shula and Robbie enjoyed a unique relationship. Robbie took care of the business end of running the team, and Shula took care of the football end. A major reason for the success of the franchise was that each one knew his own boundaries and didn't mess with the other's turf. They understood each other, they got along with each other, and they both wanted their team to win football games.[3]

Leadership

Shula was often described as football's "winningest coach." His talent was in getting his players to perform to their maximum potential.

Ken Blanchard, author of *The One Minute Manager*, observed in describing Shula, that "some coaches . . . are players' coaches; they want the team to love them. Don doesn't care if they like him. That is not his job. His concern is that players be their best."[4]

Don Strock, a former Dolphins quarterback, reinforced that observation, saying that Shula "always had the knack and the ability to bring out the best in his players whether they were superstars or average

The Miami Dolphins Football Team

*D*on Shula (right) is pictured here with star quarterback Bob Griese. In Shula's first year as head coach he led the Dolphins to their first winning season.

talents." In other words, in order to get the best out of each person, Shula allowed each player to do what he did best.[5]

Disappointments

Shula continued to lead his teams to playoff games and AFC championships, amassing an impressive number of wins along the way. Inexplicably, however, even though he brought the Dolphins to two more Super Bowls, XVII and XIX, he was never able to recapture the NFL championship.

In the 1986 through 1989 seasons, the Dolphins fell into a slump in which Shula experienced his worst four consecutive years of play in Miami: two even

Building the Team

*T*he Dolphins celebrate as Don Shula wins his 325th game. That win gave him more victories than any other coach in NFL history.

records (8-8 each), one losing (6-10), and one barely winning (8-7).[6]

The 1990s

The 1990 season was a successful one. The Dolphins not only had a winning year, 12-4, they also won their first-round playoff game against the Kansas City Chiefs, 17–16. Then they lost their divisional playoff against the Buffalo Bills, 44–34. Unfortunately, the ensuing years did not see any resurgence of the old Dolphins. They won an occasional playoff, but they just couldn't seem to make it to the AFC championship. When they did manage to get there, in 1992, they lost to Buffalo, 29–10.[7]

Good-bye, Coach

On January 6, 1996, Don Shula retired from coaching. Thirty-three years after succeeding Weeb Eubank as coach of the Baltimore Colts in 1963, the living legend stepped down, not in the spirit of defeat, but in the manner of a proud warrior who has fought the noble fight and has been victorious.

Upon Shula's retirement, NFL Commissioner Paul Tagliabue said, "Don Shula represents the highest standards of excellence by virtually any measure. His contributions to the NFL extend far beyond his victory total."[8] In 1997, his first year of eligibility, Shula was elected to the Professional Football Hall of Fame.

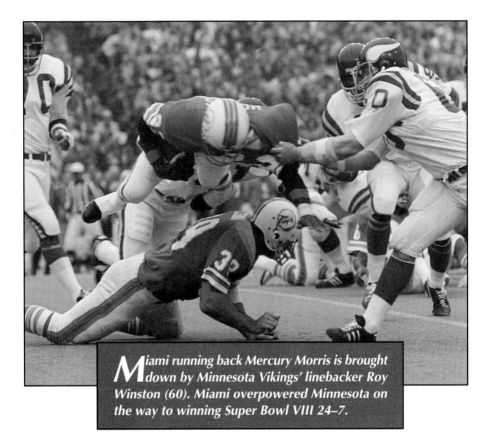

Miami running back Mercury Morris is brought down by Minnesota Vikings' linebacker Roy Winston (60). Miami overpowered Minnesota on the way to winning Super Bowl VIII 24–7.

HIGHLIGHTS

While the 1972 season will remain the single most spectacular season in Miami history, the team did have other banner years. In thirty years of existence, the Dolphins played in five Super Bowls, each one representing an outstanding season.

Super Bowls VI–VIII

Overwhelmed by Dallas 24–3 in Super Bowl VI, the Dolphins returned in 1972 to Super Bowl VII, making NFL history in the process. Ending the 1973 season 12-2 gave Miami the best two-year record, 26-2, in modern NFL history. Excitement was high when the Dolphins won their second consecutive Super Bowl, this time against the Minnesota Vikings, 24–7.

The Dry Years

Unfortunately, it would be nine years before Miami made another Super Bowl appearance. During that period, the Dolphins experienced some major player changes.

The Dolphins were caught off guard when Csonka, Warfield, and Kiick announced that they were leaving to join Toronto in the newly formed World Football League. Their departure hurt Miami.

Because of a dispute with Shula, Jake Scott, the team's all-time interception leader, was suspended, then traded. In one season alone, eighteen players were sidelined because of injuries. In addition, between Super Bowls, Morrall, Little, and Griese retired.[1]

Back in the Game

The 1982 preseason and first two weeks of the regular season were filled with tension because of talk of an impending players' strike. The Dolphins won their first two games before the strike went into effect. The NFL was idle for a total of fifty-seven days,[2] causing Miami to miss seven games.[3]

During the strike, a nucleus of about thirty-eight Dolphins stayed together as a team, working out and practicing. By the time the strike was over, the Dolphins, because of their daily workouts, were in better shape than the teams that had not practiced.[4]

The Dolphins finished the season 7-2, qualifying them to play in the first round of the AFC playoffs. They beat the New England Patriots, 28–13, then they went on to win the second round against the San Diego Chargers, 34–13.

The Dolphins were now ready to take on the New York Jets for the AFC championship. Winning 14–0,

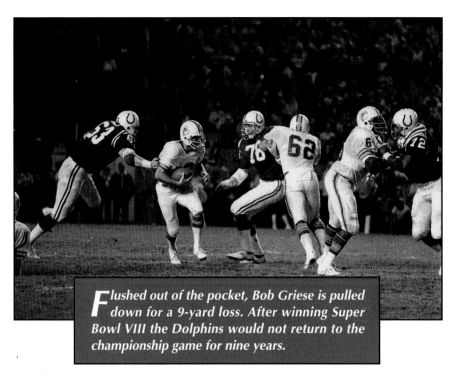

*F*lushed out of the pocket, Bob Griese is pulled down for a 9-yard loss. After winning Super Bowl VIII the Dolphins would not return to the championship game for nine years.

Miami set an AFC championship game record by holding the Jets to 139 total yards.[5]

Super Bowl XVII

Having disposed of all the AFC competition, the Dolphins were now ready to face the powerful Redskins in Super Bowl XVII, the game they had been waiting for since Super Bowl VIII.

The Dolphins jumped to a quick lead in the first quarter and led the Redskins at the half, 17–10. In the fourth period, with 10:01 left in the game, Washington came from behind and took the lead for the first time. On a short-yardage play, Redskin John Riggins broke a tackle and scored on a 43-yard run. Mark Mosely's

*T*he Miami Dolphins faced the San Francisco 49ers in Super Bowl XIX. San Francisco crushed the Dolphins 38–16.

successful kick put Washington ahead, 20–17. With 1:55 left to play, the Redskins scored another TD, making the final score 27–17. The defeat was a crushing blow for Miami.[6]

Super Bowl XIX

In 1984, Miami once again had a winning season, 14-2. Facing the Seattle Seahawks in the AFC playoffs, the Dolphins won, 31–10. Miami then faced the Pittsburgh Steelers for the AFC championship. Led by Dan Marino's 421 yards passing and Mark Duper's 148 yards receiving, the Dolphins soundly trounced the Steelers, 45–28, paving the way to Super Bowl XIX.[7]

As in Super Bowl XVII, Miami could not pull everything together. The San Francisco 49ers, led by quarterback Joe Montana, were just too much for the Dolphins. Outplayed and outgained, Miami and lost Super Bowl XIX, 38–16.[8]

Other Playoffs and Championships

Between Super Bowls VIII and XVII, and the one season between XVII and XIX, the Dolphins made it to playoff games five times without advancing to the championship. There were six years in which they didn't even make it to a playoff game. Of the five years in which they did get to the playoffs, they advanced to the AFC championship twice, losing both times. What a comedown for the once mighty Dolphins!

In January 1994, Wayne Huizenga became the sole owner of the Miami Dolphins and Joe Robbie Stadium.

DOLPHINS TODAY

n March 1990, two months after Joe Robbie's death, Wayne Huizenga, a highly successful businessman, bought into the Miami Dolphins and the Joe Robbie Stadium. He became sole owner of both in January 1994.[1]

The $18 Million Cure

A big Shula fan, Huizenga had high hopes for the team. In preparation for the 1995 season, he gave Shula free rein to spend more than $18 million in signing bonuses. With nineteen former first-round draft choices on the roster, expectations were high that this "star power" team would burn up the AFC and go on to win that elusive Super Bowl.[2]

Although the Dolphins started strong, 9-7 was the best they could do for the season. Barely good enough to rate a wildcard slot, the team was not good enough to beat Buffalo in the first-round playoffs. The

Dolphins' defeat, 37–22, was just too demoralizing to be accepted stoically. This, apparently, was the straw that broke the camel's back.

What Went Wrong?

How could Don Shula, the winningest coach in football, not field another victorious Super Bowl team in over twenty years?

After the disappointing 1995 season, sportswriters offered some astute, as well as obvious, explanations. One attributed the problems to "out-of-whackness," explaining that miscalculations were made at the top in thinking the best players could be bought and expected to function as a team.[3]

Another writer stated that it doesn't matter how talented the player is, he has to "fit." You cannot just buy high-priced talented players and expect them to function as a team unless they fit.[4] A glaring example was tight end Eric Green, who was underutilized and was not allowed to do what he did best—blocking.[5]

Yet another pundit proclaimed, "If Don Shula didn't insist on being his own general manager, who brought in a herd of Trojan horses disguised as pricey free agents, he could have won as long as he could breathe."[6]

The End of an Era

Amid such widespread criticism, when Don Shula announced his retirement, the decision was met with joy, hope, and anticipation, but also with regret and sadness.

The Miami Dolphins Football Team

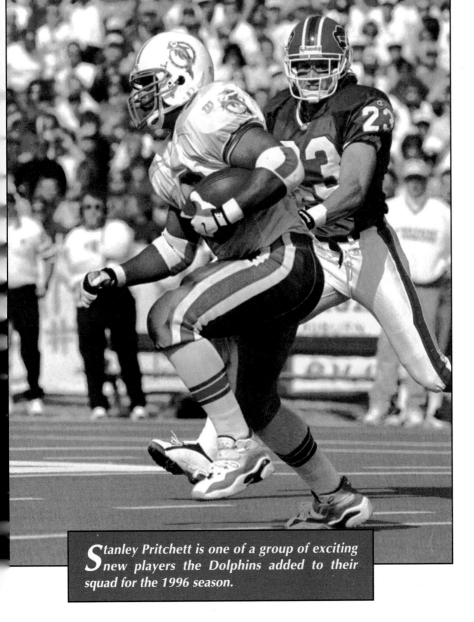

*S*tanley Pritchett is one of a group of exciting new players the Dolphins added to their squad for the 1996 season.

With one year left on his contract, Shula conceded that a lame duck coach would find it impossible to hire additional coaching staff for just one year. So Shula, ever the honorable and dedicated coach, put the good of the team ahead of his own desires to win one more Super Bowl, and stepped down.

The winningest coach in NFL history was calling it a day, proving that even legends lose their luster. Even so, nothing can diminish the brilliance of his accomplishments. The records he set will stand far into the future.

Ring in the New

Not wanting to waste valuable time, Huizenga signed up Jimmy Johnson as coach. A local legend himself, Johnson had coached the University of Miami Hurricanes to a national championship in 1987.[7]

It was his ability as coach of the Dallas Cowboys that made Johnson a desirable successor to Shula. Just as Shula had taken the Dolphins from loser status to back-to-back Super Bowl victories, Johnson had taken Dallas from 1-15 in his first season in 1989 to consecutive Super Bowl victories in 1992 and 1993.[8]

High Hopes

General reaction to Johnson, only the third coach in Miami's history, is one of approval, confidence, and anticipation. Expectations are high that Johnson will work the miracle Miami has been anxiously awaiting for more than twenty years: a Super Bowl victory.

*J*immy Johnson cheers his team on. After Shula's retirement, Johnson, who led the Dallas Cowboys to two Super Bowl victories, became the Dolphins head coach for the 1996 season.

Johnson's first actions involved hiring support personnel and coaching staff. Decisions about which players to retain or let go would be made later—except for one. Amid speculation that Johnson might trade the spectacular Dan Marino, Johnson squelched that rumor when he said he was looking forward to coaching the star quarterback.[9]

As for Johnson's reaction to being named Miami coach, he couldn't be happier. What does he expect to accomplish? "I expect success and that's what I'm going to work to get."[10]

Miami fans everywhere are hoping he will.

STATISTICS

Team Record

SEASON	SEASON RECORD	PLAYOFF RECORD	COACH	DIVISION FINISH
1966	3-11	—	George Wilson	4th (tie)
1967	4-10	—	George Wilson	3rd (tie)
1968	5-8-1	—	George Wilson	3rd
1969	3-10-1	—	George Wilson	5th
1970	10-4	0-1	Don Shula	2nd
1971	10-3-1	2-1	Don Shula	1st
1972	14-0	3-0	Don Shula	1st
1973	12-2	3-0	Don Shula	1st
1974	11-3	0-1	Don Shula	1st
1975	10-4	—	Don Shula	2nd
1976	6-8	—	Don Shula	3rd
1977	10-4	—	Don Shula	2nd
1978	11-5	0-1	Don Shula	2nd
1979	10-6	0-1	Don Shula	1st
1980	8-8	—	Don Shula	3rd
1981	11-4-1	0-1	Don Shula	1st
1982	7-2	3-1	Don Shula	2nd (tie)
1983	12-4	0-1	Don Shula	1st
1984	14-2	2-1	Don Shula	1st
1985	12-4	1-1	Don Shula	1st
1986	8-8	—	Don Shula	3rd

The Miami Dolphins Football Team

Team Record (con't)

SEASON	SEASON RECORD	PLAYOFF RECORD	COACH	DIVISION FINISH
1987	8-7	—	Don Shula	2nd (tie)
1988	6-10	—	Don Shula	5th
1989	8-8	—	Don Shula	2nd (tie)
1990	12-4	1-1	Don Shula	2nd
1991	8-8	—	Don Shula	2nd (tie)
1992	11-5	1-1	Don Shula	1st
1993	9-7	—	Don Shula	2nd
1994	10-6	1-1	Don Shula	1st
1995	9-7	0-1	Don Shula	2nd
1996	8-8	—	Jimmy Johnson	4th
Totals	280-180-4	17-14	Jimmy Johnson	4th

Coaching Records

COACH	SEASONS	RECORD	CHAMPIONSHIPS
George Wilson	1966–69	15-39-2	None
Don Shula	1970–95	257-133-2	AFC Eastern Division Champions, 1974, 1979, 1981, 1983, 1985, 1992, 1994 AFC Champions, 1971, 1982, 1984 Super Bowl VII, VIII
Jimmy Johnson	1996–	8-8	None

Statistics

Great Dolphins' Career Statistics

PASSING

PLAYER	SEASONS	Y	G	ATT	COMP	YDS	TD
*Bob Griese	1967–80	14	161	3,429	1,926	25,092	192
Dan Marino	1983–	14	199	6,904	4,134	51,636	369
Earl Morrall	1972–76	21	255	2,689	1,379	20,809	161

RUSHING

PLAYER	SEASONS	Y	G	ATT	YDS	AVG	TD
*Larry Csonka	1968–74, 1979	11	146	1,891	8,081	4.3	64
Jim Kiick	1968–74	9	115	1,029	3,763	3.7	29

RECEIVING

PLAYER	SEASONS	Y	G	REC	YDS	AVG	TD
Mark Clayton	1983–92	11	158	582	8,974	15.4	84
*Paul Warfield	1970–74	13	164	427	8,565	20.1	85

KICKING

PLAYER	SEASONS	Y	G	FG	XP	TOTAL POINTS
Garo Yepremian	1970–78	14	177	210	444	1,074

DEFENSE

PLAYER	SEASONS	Y	G	TACK	AST	TOT	SACK	INT	FUM
Bryan Cox	1991–95	6	86	476	160	636	34.5	3	8

OFFENSIVE LINE

PLAYER	SEASONS	Y	G	ACCOMPLISHMENTS
*Larry Little	1969–80	14	158	All-Pro Selection, 1971–75, 1977; Offensive Lineman of the Year, 1970–72

*Hall of Fame Members

SEASONS=Seasons with Dolphins
Y=Years in the NFL
G=Games
ATT=Attempts
YDS=Yards

COMP=Completions
AVG=Average
TD=Touchdowns
REC=Receptions
FG=Field Goals
XP=Extra Points

TACK=Tackles
AST=Assists
TOT=Total
SACK=Sacks
INT=Interceptions
FUM=Fumble Recoveries

The Miami Dolphins Football Team

CHAPTER NOTES

Chapter 1

1. Harvey Greene, Scott Stone, and Mike Hanson, *Miami Dolphins 1995 Media Guide* (Miami: The Franklin Press, 1995), p. 414.

2. Bill Gutman, *Football Super Teams* (New York: Pocket Books, 1991), p. 59.

3. Gutman, pp. 60–61.

4. Greene et al., p. 414.

Chapter 2

1. Beau Riffenburgh, ed. *The Official NFL Encyclopedia*, 4th ed., (New York: New American Library, 1986), p. 135.

2. Harvey Greene, Scott Stone, and Mike Hanson, *Miami Dolphins 1995 Media Guide* (Miami: The Franklin Press, 1995), p. 304.

3. Riffenburgh, p. 136.

4. George Sullivan, *Pro Football A to Z* (New York: Winchester Press, 1975), p. 269.

5. Riffenburgh, p. 136.

6. Greene et al., p. 410.

7. Larry Csonka, Jim Kiick, and Dave Anderson, *Always on the Run* (New York: Random House, 1973), p. 196.

Chapter 3

1. Bill Gutman, *Football Super Teams* (New York: Pocket Books, 1991), p. 48.

2. Harvey Greene, Scott Stone, and Mike Hanson. *Miami Dolphins 1995 Media Guide* (Miami: The Franklin Press, 1995), p. 459.

3. Gutman, p. 47.

4. Greene et al., p. 458.

5. Larry Csonka, Jim Kiick, and Dave Anderson, *Always on the Run* (New York: Random House, 1973), p. 49.

Chapter 4

1. Beau Riffenburgh, ed. *The Official NFL Encyclopedia* 4th ed. (New York: New American Library, 1986), p. 135.

2. Office of Media Relations, *Miami Dolphins 1990 Media Guide* (Miami: Miami Dolphins, 1990), p. 8.

3. Don Strock, and Harvey Frommer, *Behind the Lines* (New York: Pharos Books, 1991), pp. 31–32.

4. Don Shula, and Ken Blanchard, *Everyone's a Coach* (Grand Rapids, Mich: Harper Business, 1995), p. 53.

5. Strock and Frommer, p. 213.

6. Riffenburgh, p. 310.

7. Ibid., pp. 311–312.

8. Armando Saiguero, "Shula's Exit Opens Door for JJ," *The Herald*, Miami, January 6, 1996, p. 9D.

Chapter 5

1. Beau Riffenburgh, ed., *The Official NFL Encyclopedia*, 4th edition (New York: New American Library, 1986), p. 136.

2. Don Strock, and Harvey Frommer, *Behind the Lines* (New York: Pharos Books, 1991), pp. 106–107.

3. Harvey Greene, Scott Stone, and Mike Hanson, *Miami Dolphins 1995 Media Guide* (Miami: The Franklin Press, 1995), p. 308.

4. Strock and Frommer, p. 108.

5. Greene et al., pp. 420–421.

6. Ibid., p. 422.

7. Ibid., p. 424.

8. Ibid., p. 425.

Chapter 6

1. Harvey Greene, Scott Stone, and Mike Hanson, *Miami Dolphins 1995 Media Guide* (Miami: The Franklin Press, 1995), p. 5.

2. Steven Wine, "Shula Feeling Miami Heat," *The Times-Union* (Jacksonville, Fla.), November 28, 1995, p. D5.

3. Edwin Pope, "Title Shot Over for Dream Team," *The Herald* (Miami), October 23, 1995, p. 12D.

4. John Oehser, "Misfits Are Not Paying Off," *The Times-Union* (Jacksonville, Fla.), December 10, 1995, p. C 17.

5. Jason Cole, "Running Eludes Dolphins," *The Times-Union* (Jacksonville, Fla.), December 22, 1995, p. C9.

6. Jonathon Rand, "It Was Time for Shula to Go," *The Herald* (Miami), January 6, 1966, p. 7D.

7. Clark Spencer, and Armando Saiguero, "EX-UM Coach, Dolphins Talk," *The Herald* (Miami), January 6, 1996, p. 14A.

8. Ibid., p. 14A.

9. Shawn Oehser, "Johnson Thrilled To Coach Dolphins," *The Times-Union* (Jacksonville, Fla.), January 12, 1996, p. C4.

10. Ibid., p. C4.

The Miami Dolphins Football Team

GLOSSARY

AFL—American Football League. The AFL was a competitor of the NFL until the two leagues merged for the 1970 season.

defensive backs—The group of players consisting of the cornerbacks and safeties that guard the opposing team's wide receivers. They are the last line of defense before the end zone.

defensive linemen—The group of defensemen that line up directly at the line of scrimmage. Defensive linemen are usually made up of the nose tackle, the defensive tackles, and defensive ends.

draft—The system by which amateur athletes, usually college players, are chosen to go to a certain team. In the NFL, the team that finishes with the worst record in the regular season gets to choose first.

free agent—A player whose current contract has run out, and is now allowed to sign with any team that player chooses.

interception—This occurs when a defenseman catches a pass that was intended for an offensive player.

lame-duck coach—A coach who is in the last year of his contract with the team for which he is currently coaching.

linebackers—The players who line up behind the defensive linemen. They are responsible for stopping running backs who have gone past the defensive linemen and for covering running backs and tight ends when they go out for passes.

offensive linemen—The group of offensemen who line up at the line of scrimmage, and whose job it is to stop the defensemen from getting to the person with the ball.

playoffs—Series of games that take place between the teams with the best regular season records to determine who the NFL champion is. The playoffs are often called the postseason.

Pro-Bowl—A game that takes place after the playoffs have ended in which the best players from the National Football Conference play against the best players from the American Football Conference.

rookies—First-year players.

wild-card—The first round of the NFL playoffs.

FURTHER READING

Allen, George, and Ben Olan. *Pro Football's 100 Greatest Players*. Indianapolis/New York: The Bobbs-Merrill Co., 1982.

Anderson, Dave. *Great Quarterbacks of the NFL* rev. ed. New York: Random House, 1965.

Burchard, S. H. *Bob Griese*. New York and London: Harcourt Brace Jovanovich, 1975.

Dunnahoo, Terry Janson, and Herman Silverstein. *The Pro Football Hall of Fame*. New York: Crestwood House, 1994.

Hasegawa, Sam. *The Coaches*. Mankato, Minn: Creative Education, 1975.

———. *The Quarterbacks*. Mankato, Minn: Creative Education, 1975.

Herskowitz, Mickey. *The Quarterbacks*. New York: William Morrow & Co., 1990.

Kowet, Don. *Golden Toes: Football's Greatest Kickers*. New York: St. Martin's Press, 1972.

Sahadi, Lou. *Miracle in Miami*. Chicago: Henry Regnery Co., 1972.

Thorn, John. *Pro Football's Ten Greatest Games*. New York: Four Winds Press, 1981.

The Miami Dolphins Football Team

INDEX

WHERE TO WRITE

Miami Dolphins
7500 SW 30th Street
Davie, FL 33314

WEBSITE

http://www.pwr.com/dolphins/